The Tri-Justice System in Action
My Personal Journey Through Legal Pluralism in 15 BARMM Barangays

Mansoor Limba

The Tri-Justice System in Action: My Personal Journey Though Legal Pluralism in 15 BARMM Barangays

Copyright © 2025 Mansoor Limba, PhD, SCL

All rights reserved.

ISBN: 9798340407122

Published by
ElziStyle Bookshop
#66 Sousa Extension, Rosary Heights 12,
Cotabato City, Philippines

Cover Design and Photo by Mansoor Limba

All rights reserved. No part of this work or publication may be reproduced, stored in a retrieval system, or transmitted, in any form or by any means, without the prior permission of the copyright holder.

Any trademarks, service marks, product names or named features are assumed to be the property of their respective owners and are used only for reference. There is no implied endorsement if one of these terms is used here.

DEDICATION

Dedicated to my Roommate, Leilali, and our ever-baby daughter, Lady Zaynab, for wholeheartedly overlooking my lapses of both omission and commission as a roomie and sitter, respectively.

CONTENTS

	Dedication	
	Foreword	1
Prologue	Unveiling the Tri-Justice System in BARMM	5
1	Let's Meet Commander Scientist of Fukol	11
2	A Heartbeat of Peace Called 'Kaya-Kaya'	17
3	For Kauran, It's Restoration and Healing	23
4	The Symbolic Fragility of Bungcog's Chicken Egg	29
5	The Tree of Life and Peace in Rempes	35
6	Moriatao Loksadatu's 4Ks of Settlement	41
7	Rantian's Tapestry of Tradition, Faith, and Governance	47
8	Poblacion VII's Silt Island of Tri-Justice System	53
9	Tumbras' Seeds of Justice and Harmony	59
10	Lamion's Pathway to Community Harmony	65
11	Tubig-Boh's Conflict Resolution with Heart	72
12	Walking Around Like a Native in Bongao	77
13	Sulu Mysteries of a Proud Past	83
14	Modern *Langgal* as Bilaan's Heart of Peace	89
15	If Only Astana Could Speak	95
16	Bus-Bus – Where Neighbors Mend and Peace Endures	99
17	Tumahubong's Voices of Resolution	105
18	For Malinis, It's Carefully Crafted	109

Epilogue	Retracing 3 Pillars of Barangay Justice in BARMM	115
	About the Author	**121**
	Other Books by the Author	123
	Connect with the Author	126

FOREWORD

At ElziStyle Bookshop, we are honored to present this groundbreaking work, *The Tri-Justice System in Action: My Personal Journey Through Legal Pluralism in 15 BARMM Barangays* by Mansoor Limba.

This book is a profound exploration of the unique and intricate tri-justice system practiced in the Bangsamoro Autonomous Region in Muslim Mindanao (BARMM), offering readers an insightful perspective on how traditional, civil, and religious justice systems coexist and function at the grassroots level.

Mansoor Limba brings a wealth of expertise and experience to this work. As a university professor teaching subjects related to conflict resolution, legal pluralism, and Shari'ah, Limba is deeply immersed in the academic and practical aspects of these topics. He

THE TRI-JUSTICE SYSTEM IN ACTION: MY PERSONAL JOURNEY THROUGH LEGAL PLURALISM IN 15 BARMM BARANGAYS

is also an alumnus of Clingendael (Netherlands Institute of International Relations), where he trained on Negotiation and Mediation in Conflict Resolution, and a Shariʻah Counselor-at-Law (SCL). With his rich background, Limba offers a nuanced analysis of how different justice systems—Islamic, tribal, and civil—work together to resolve disputes in the BARMM barangays.

In this book, Limba takes readers on a personal journey through 15 barangays, each with its own unique culture and legal traditions. His firsthand accounts provide not only scholarly analysis but also an intimate look into the lives of the Moro, Non-Moro Indigenous Peoples (NMIPs), and Christian settlers who make up the tri-people composition of the region.

Through the lens of legal pluralism, Limba uncovers how these communities balance Islamic law, traditional customs, and the national justice system to create a unique form of governance centered on peace, reconciliation, and social harmony.

More than just a study of legal frameworks, this book captures the voices, wisdom, and stories of the barangay leaders, elders, and Lupong Tagapamayapa members who work tirelessly to uphold justice.

Limba's personal reflections on the tri-justice system reveal the challenges and successes of integrating diverse legal traditions, while also showcasing the resilience and adaptability of the people in the Bangsamoro in navigating this complex system.

We are also pleased to publish *The Tri-Justice System in Action* in celebration of the first anniversary of the passage of the Bangsamoro Local Governance Code (BLGC) by the Bangsamoro Parliament on September 28, 2023, and its approval on the same day by the Interim Chief Minister Ahod B. Ebrahim.

This book serves as a timely contribution to the region's evolving governance framework, showcasing how local justice systems work to maintain peace, social order, and resilience across diverse communities in the BARMM.

The Tri-Justice System in Action is an essential resource for anyone interested in legal pluralism, conflict resolution, and peacebuilding. It offers valuable insights into the justice system of the BARMM and provides a model for how multiple legal systems can coexist to maintain social harmony.

Limba's background as a professor, Shari'ah counselor, and expert in conflict mediation enriches this work, giving readers a deep understanding of how negotiation and mediation are applied to real-world conflicts.

At ElziStyle Bookshop, we believe in sharing stories that matter—stories that highlight diversity, resilience, and the pursuit of justice.

We are proud to bring this work to readers across the world and invite you to join Mansoor Limba on

THE TRI-JUSTICE SYSTEM IN ACTION: MY PERSONAL JOURNEY THROUGH LEGAL PLURALISM IN 15 BARMM BARANGAYS

his personal journey through the tri-justice system of BARMM.

Elzistyle Bookshop
September 28, 2024 ☪

*****

Prologue

UNVEILING THE TRI-JUSTICE SYSTEM IN BARMM

In the Name of Allah,

the All-just, the All-forgiving

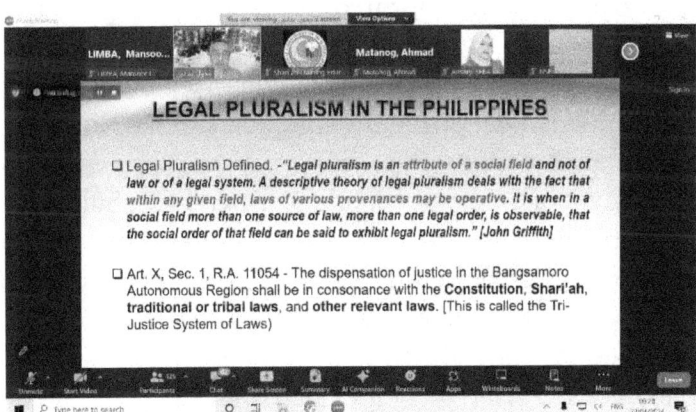

Sometimes, the most transformative journeys begin in the most unexpected ways.

THE TRI-JUSTICE SYSTEM IN ACTION: MY PERSONAL JOURNEY THROUGH LEGAL PLURALISM IN 15 BARMM BARANGAYS

It was just two short months after Atty. Mehol Sadain delivered his thought-provoking review lecture on the tri-justice system in the Philippines' pluralistic legal framework.

This was part of our "Court Procedure" Shari'ah Bar Exam preparation last April. What I initially approached as an academic endeavor quickly took on a life of its own, morphing into a hands-on exploration that would lead me deep into the heart of the Bangsamoro Autonomous Region in Muslim Mindanao (BARMM).

Little did I know, I was about to embark on a journey that would open my eyes to the intricate ways in which traditional, religious, and civil laws intertwine at the grassroots level.

Over the course of three weeks, I traveled through 15 barangays—each one unique, ranging from the marshy lowlands and mountainous terrains of Maguindanao del Sur and Maguindanao del Norte, to the vibrant communities of Cotabato City, and the distant yet picturesque islands of Tawi-Tawi, Sulu, and Basilan, including the bustling Lamitan City. Each stop on this unexpected journey was like peeling back layers of a complex legal and cultural system, offering glimpses into how the tri-justice system operates in the daily lives of Moro, Non-Moro Indigenous Peoples (NMIPs), and Christian settlers.

In one barangay, an elder spoke passionately about the traditional practices that still guide their conflict resolutions. "We've done this for generations," he said, as we sat under the shade of a towering tree. "Here, we swear on the Qur'an, through the practice of *yamin* (swearing), to resolve disputes. It's more than a legal procedure—it's a binding oath to Allah."

In other barangays, the challenges were different, but the passion was the same. In certain barangays, the Lupong Tagapamayapa (Conciliation Council) shared their struggle in mediating disputes involving Shari'ah laws. "Sometimes, we don't know how far we can go," admitted one council member. "Marital issues, for instance—we know it's not under our jurisdiction, but people still come to us for help."

This recurring confusion highlights a significant gap in the system. While traditional methods like *yamin* are still widely respected, there is a pressing need for greater clarity in how the various legal systems intersect. That's why the creation or organization of Shari'ah Public Assistance Offices (SPAO) is so critical. As one official remarked during a focused group discussion in Tawi-Tawi, "With an SPAO in every municipality, we could register marriages and divorces easily. Imagine the burden we could lift off people's shoulders if we could settle disputes faster."

Through the mix of focus group discussions and observations, several key themes emerged:

General Observations:

1. The 15 barangays being selected for visitation reflect all possible tri-people combination of barangay

constituencies: Moro (Maguindanaon) and IPs (Teduray) (Brgy. Fukol), purely Moro (Maguindanaon, Iranun, Maranao, Tausug, Sama, or Yakan) (Brgy. Kaya-Kaya, Brgy. Moriatao Luksadato, Brgy. Rantian, Brgy. Bilaan, Brgy. Tumahubong), overwhelmingly Christian settlers and some IPs (Brgy. Kauran), majority Moro and some Christian settlers (Brgy. Poblacion 7, Brgy. Tumbras), overwhelmingly IPs and Christian settlers and Moro (Brgy. Bungcog), majority Christian settlers and some IPs and Moro (Brgy. Rempes, Brgy. Malinis), majority Moro and some Christian settlers and IPs (Brgy. Lamion and Brgy. Tubig-Boh). Thus, a tri-justice system is observed accordingly.

2. Traditional Conflict Resolution: Traditional ways of resolving disputes, such as the swearing of oaths on the Qur'an, are still widely practiced in areas where the Moro and NMIP populations are dominant.

3. Jurisdictional Confusion: Despite the continued use of these traditional practices, there remains confusion among the Lupong Tagapamayapa in handling certain cases—particularly marital disputes, which are technically outside their jurisdiction.

One Lupon member from another barangay said it best: "We know the old ways, and we respect them, but the law is always changing. We need help keeping up."

The solution lies in better support for the communities. The Bangsamoro Organic Law (Article

X, Section 16) has already provided a foundation for this, outlining the creation of Shari'ah Public Assistance Offices in each municipality. These offices would not only streamline processes like marriage and divorce registrations but also provide clear legal guidance for the Lupong Tagapamayapa. By doing so, the complex web of the tri-justice system can be navigated more effectively, ensuring that both tradition and law are upheld in a harmonious balance.

As my journey came to an end, I realized that what I had uncovered was not just a complex system of justice, but a living, breathing tapestry of law, culture, and faith. The tri-justice system, though nuanced and sometimes difficult to navigate, is deeply ingrained in the lives of the people of BARMM. It serves as a testament to the region's resilience and its commitment to maintaining harmony amidst diversity.

The road ahead requires support and refinement, but one thing is certain: true justice here is not just about legal rulings—it's about respect, understanding, and the pursuit of peace at every level.

*****

Story 1
LET'S MEET COMMANDER SCIENTIST OF FUKOL

The journey of a thousand miles, they say, begins with a single step.

For me, that step was into the remote barangays of the Bangsamoro Autonomous Region in Muslim

THE TRI-JUSTICE SYSTEM IN ACTION: MY PERSONAL JOURNEY THROUGH LEGAL PLURALISM IN 15 BARMM BARANGAYS

Mindanao (BARMM), where I would explore the applications of the barangay tri-justice system.

My first stop: Barangay Fukol, nestled in the mountains of Talayan Municipality, Maguindanao del Sur.

It was a bright morning as our Ministry of the Interior and Local Government (MILG) team set off from Cotabato City, heading towards Talayan Municipal Hall for a courtesy call. The town mayor, a high school batchmate of mine, greeted us warmly. After exchanging pleasantries and shortly reminiscing about our school days, we were back on the road for the final 20-minute drive to Barangay Fukol.

The smooth, paved road exceeded my expectations, and soon, we found ourselves pulling into the barangay, greeted by the sight of a welcoming committee led by the young barangay chairman. His energy was palpable as he introduced us to the Lupong Tagapamayapa (Conciliation Council) members, about 20 in total, who had gathered for our focus group discussion (FGD).

As we settled in, a strong handshake from Datucon Watamama, an elder of the Lupon, nearly caught me off guard. This man, I quickly learned, was better known as "Commander Scientist," a name that resonated with a mix of respect and curiosity. Before I could ask about the origin of his unique title, he began to share stories from his days as the 8th Battalion Commander of the Inner Guard Base

STORY 1

Command of the Moro Islamic Liberation Front (MILF).

"Thirty years in these mountains," he began, his voice rich with the weight of experience, "and I've seen this barangay transform from a simple, isolated community to the multi-award-winning barangay it is today."

I listened intently, sipping on the hot native coffee they offered, its warmth complemented by the fresh boiled banana and camote on the table. Commander Scientist's tales were mesmerizing, each word painting a vivid picture of the struggles and triumphs of a community that had seen both conflict and peace.

Our conversation soon shifted to the reason for my visit: the barangay's unique mediation processes. As Commander Scientist spoke, the young barangay chairman and other Lupon members, both Maguindanaon and Teduray, nodded in agreement, their respect for the elder evident.

"Here in Barangay Fukol," he explained, "we blend tradition with practicality. Our methods are rooted in our culture and our faith."

He went on to describe the various techniques they employed during mediation:

Counseling: "We start by speaking calmly to each party, ensuring they present their sides with the same calmness during the settlement."

THE TRI-JUSTICE SYSTEM IN ACTION: MY PERSONAL JOURNEY THROUGH LEGAL PLURALISM IN 15 BARMM BARANGAYS

Ablution: "Before entering the mediation hall, the disputing parties perform ablution. It purifies them, both physically and spiritually, as they prepare to take an oath."

Prayers and Invocation: "A shared prayer reminds everyone of our common humanity and our shared goal—to resolve the dispute."

Peace Advice by Elders: "The elders offer advice before mediation, using their wisdom to help the parties see beyond the immediate conflict."

Shaking Hands: "A handshake at the end symbolizes agreement and closure. It's a sign that both parties consent to the resolution."

Padlock Closure: "For disputes involving women, we lock a padlock and throw the key into a barangay-owned pan. It symbolizes the finality of the resolution."

Peace Tree Planting: "In land disputes, both parties plant trees at the boundary. It symbolizes peace, unity, and mutual respect."

Garden of Peace: "In disputes involving youth, they plant five different flowers together. It's a symbol of cooperation, diversity, and working together to create something lasting."

As our discussion deepened, our team leader gently signaled that it was time to move on to the next barangay, Barangay Kaya-Kaya in Datu Abdullah

STORY 1

Sangki Municipality. Reluctantly, I bid farewell to Commander Scientist and the others.

As our vehicle wound through the mountain roads, I found myself lost in thought, reflecting on the wisdom shared by Commander Scientist. His stories, his experiences, and the unique approaches of Barangay Fukol had left a deep impression on me.

I knew that this wouldn't be my last visit. There were more stories to uncover, more wisdom to absorb, and more cups of hot coffee to share.

Perhaps, next time, we would sit down for a longer conversation, accompanied by more of Talayan's *dinangay a saging* and a hearty serving of *linigir-a-manok* for lunch.

*****

Story 2

A HEARTBEAT OF PEACE CALLED 'KAYA-KAYA'

As the sun began to sink behind the rugged peaks of the mountains, casting long shadows over Barangay Fukol, we exchanged warm farewells with the Lupon members and barangay officials.

THE TRI-JUSTICE SYSTEM IN ACTION: MY PERSONAL JOURNEY THROUGH LEGAL PLURALISM IN 15 BARMM BARANGAYS

The air was thick with the scent of upland trees, a sharp contrast to the marshy lands that awaited us. Our mission was far from over.

From the remote highlands of Talayan, Maguindanao del Sur, our team set out on another leg of our journey—this time toward the lowland barangay of Kaya-Kaya in Datu Abdullah Sangki, where the landscape would shift from imposing hills to quiet marshes. A sense of anticipation hung in the air as we embarked on the 30-minute drive, Datu Jun's van bouncing along the municipal roads.

It was the kind of trip where every bend in the road seemed to bring a new story, a new lesson.

Half an hour later, as we cruised down the national highway, we were joined by the Municipal Local Government Operations Officer (MLGOO) and her two staff members. Their presence was a reminder that each barangay had its own intricacies, its own heartbeat.

After another 20 minutes on narrower roads, we finally arrived at Kaya-Kaya, greeted by the noon sun and the sight of barangay officials who had been waiting patiently since the early hours of the morning. Their warm smiles, despite the long wait, set the tone for the rest of our day.

As we settled down for the lunch that the barangay had graciously prepared, I found myself sitting beside a young military lieutenant. Curiosity got the better of me, and I imagined myself striking up a conversation with him. "So, what brings you to this meeting?" I asked, glancing at his uniform, a sight not commonly associated with discussions on local justice systems.

"Well," I was imagining him saying with a slight chuckle, "it might seem unusual, but considering the area we're in—so close to what's known as the SPMS Box, especially after the Mamasapano Incident back in 2015—military presence is quite necessary." He explained that he had been invited to join the focused group discussion with the Lupon members. As our conversation deepened, I learned that he was not only a military officer but also a Licensed Professional Teacher (LPT) from Cebu.

He shared that he had been stationed in the area for two years, and this was his first experience living in a predominantly Moro community. "I used to have so many misconceptions," he admitted. "But living here changed me. It changed how I see other people, how I see myself, and how I approach peace. It's no longer about enforcement, but about understanding." His words lingered in my mind, a testament to the transformative power of empathy.

After lunch, the focused discussion with the Lupon members commenced. The energy in the room was palpable as the Lupon Clerk, several members, and the Barangay Chair actively participated. They exchanged ideas with enthusiasm, sharing insights about their methods for resolving disputes. What stood out were the culturally-rooted techniques employed by the Lupong Tagapamayapa, which not only adhered to legal principles but also resonated with the community's values and spiritual beliefs.

Some of the key practices they shared included:

1. Purok Visitation: The Lupon Tagapamayapa members make regular visits to the puroks (neighborhoods) within Barangay Kaya-Kaya. These visits help them stay connected to the pulse of the community and address conflicts before they escalate.

2. Settlement Based on Maguindanaon Customary Laws (*'Adat*): They incorporate *'adat*, the traditional laws of the Maguindanaon people, into their conflict resolution processes. This ensures that the outcomes are not only legally sound but also deeply respectful of local customs.

3. Consultation with Community Elders: The wisdom of the community's elders is a key resource in resolving disputes. Their knowledge of both tradition and history provides valuable context to the mediation process.

4. Tree Planting After the Settlement: As a symbolic act of reconciliation, the Lupon encourages both parties involved in a dispute to participate in a tree-planting ceremony once the matter is resolved. This not only signifies a fresh start but also nurtures the community's connection to the land.

As we prepared to leave Kaya-Kaya, a sense of accomplishment mingled with the lingering

STORY 2

conversation about peace, tradition, and understanding. The stories shared and the techniques employed by the Lupong Tagapamayapa had opened our eyes to a unique approach to conflict resolution—one that blended the law with cultural and spiritual wisdom.

But the day wasn't over yet. With the discussion still fresh in our minds, our team was signaled to move. We had one more stop: Barangay Kauran in the neighboring municipality of Ampatuan.

As we boarded the van once again, I looked back at the village of Kaya-Kaya.

It felt as though we were leaving not just a place, but a community woven deeply with history and resilience. The road ahead was long, but it was the stories we carried with us that would make the journey unforgettable.

We were reminded that each place we visited was not just a checkpoint, but a heartbeat in the larger pulse of the province—a province seeking peace and understanding amid its complex past.

*****

Story 3

FOR KAURAN, IT'S RESTORATION AND HEALING

It was the third barangay visit of the day.

Despite the tiredness settling in, a sense of anticipation filled the air as we made our way from Barangay Kaya-Kaya in Datu Abdullah Sangki to another quiet, peaceful community of Barangay

THE TRI-JUSTICE SYSTEM IN ACTION: MY PERSONAL JOURNEY THROUGH LEGAL PLURALISM IN 15 BARMM BARANGAYS

Kauran, nestled in the town of Ampatuan, Maguindanao del Sur.

The barangay, a national awardee for its Lupong Tagapamayapa (Barangay Justice System), had a reputation that preceded it. This was a place where disputes were not just resolved but healed, where justice took the shape of reconciliation.

As we arrived, the warmth of the barangay officials and Lupon members quickly dispelled any weariness. The lady Municipal Local Government Operations Officer (MLGOO) who had joined us smiled broadly as she introduced us to the team. "Welcome to Barangay Kauran," the barangay chairman said, shaking my hand firmly. "We're honored by your visit."

I smiled and began by explaining the purpose of our visit. "We're here to write a manual on the BARMM barangay justice system," I said. "But let me make one thing clear – I'm not the author of this manual. You are. You are the experts, and I'm just here to listen, to learn, and to document your wisdom."

A few Lupon members nodded, and the chairman smiled, his eyes filled with pride. "Well, let's get started, then. We'll show you how we do things here."

As they demonstrated the process, each step was explained in detail by the Lupon members, all eager to share their approach. The chairman would begin with

STORY 3

a prayer, invoking guidance from the Almighty. "Before anything else, we ask for divine intervention," he said, his hands clasped in front of him. "This is more than just a legal process for us. It's about restoring peace, and that requires more than laws – it requires grace."

The sincerity in his voice was striking, and as the Lupon members elaborated, the true depth of their justice system began to unfold. One of the Lupon members, a woman in her mid-forties, spoke up. "We always listen to both sides with an open heart. Sometimes, emotions run high, and we have a special place – the Balay Pahuwayan – where we send those who need to calm down. It's a peaceful space with soft music, a place for reflection. When they return, they're ready to talk, not fight."

"And then there's the *Bubon Sang Pagpinasayluhanay*," the chairman added, a twinkle in his eye. "It's our Well of Forgiveness. We ask both parties to write down their anger and throw it into the well, symbolizing the release of all negative emotions." He paused, looking at me to see if I understood the significance. "It's not enough to settle disputes; we have to heal them."

Another Lupon member chimed in, her voice full of enthusiasm. "We even ask them to write a 'Letter of Friendship' after the settlement. It's a promise to remember the good times they shared before the conflict. If things go wrong again, they can read that letter and remind themselves of what they once valued."

As I listened, it became clear that Barangay Kauran's approach to justice was not just about resolving conflicts – it was about building lasting peace. This was not a process of winners and losers but of reconciliation and understanding.

One of the barangay officials mentioned the challenges of land disputes, pointing to a chart hanging on the wall. "That's our land dispute process," she said proudly. "We created it after years of dealing with these issues. It's helped us settle even the most complicated cases."

I studied the chart, impressed by their initiative. "How did you come up with this?" I asked.

"Through experience," she said with a knowing smile. "You deal with enough land disputes, and you learn what works and what doesn't."

As the afternoon wore on, we were served with their signature merienda, a delicious spread of local delicacies. It was a moment of calm before our departure, and I couldn't help but glance at their new barangay hall under construction. Or rather, not under construction. The work had clearly been halted, leaving the building incomplete.

"Why did the construction stop?" I wondered aloud as we prepared to leave. "Budget issues? Or maybe the contractor's fault?"

STORY 3

I couldn't shake the thought as we boarded the van. "Why not hold the contractor accountable? Why not take it to task? Why not ban the contractor from all biddings of BARMM projects, if it's the contractor's fault?" These questions buzzed in my head, unanswered, as we left Barangay Kauran behind, the unfinished barangay hall a lingering symbol of unresolved issues.

But as we headed for Cotabato City, the sense of peace and community that I had witnessed stayed with me. Barangay Kauran wasn't perfect – no community is – but their approach to justice, to healing, was something special. It was more than just a process; it was a way of life, a belief in the power of forgiveness, and a commitment to making peace last.

And as I looked back at the day, I realized something: justice, in its truest form, is not about punishment. It's about restoration. It's about hope. It's about healing.

And that's a lesson we could all stand to learn.

*****

Story 4

THE SYMBOLIC FRAGILITY OF BUNGCOG'S CHICKEN EGG

The second day of our barangay visits dawned crisp and clear, with the air thick with anticipation.

After a successful first day spent in the lowland barangays of Maguindanao del Sur, today was a journey up into the highlands, to two remote barangays in Upi, Maguindanao del Norte. The rolling hills stretched before us, promising a day of discovery and connection.

Just as we began the steep ascent along the Datu Odin Sinsuat–Upi border, my phone buzzed. It was my nephew. "Bapa (Uncle) …" he said quietly. "Bapa Kagi (Uncle Hajji) Ulim returned to the mercy of the Lord early this morning in Davao City." (Kaka Ulim, an elder cousin, was a deputy base commander of the Moro Islamic Liberation Front (MILF).)

As Datu Jun gripped the steering wheel tighter, my mind whirled. Life, I thought to myself, is an inexorable web of union and separation, of arrivals and departures. The Divine decree had called him home. There, on the winding mountain road, I submitted to the reality of it all.

After an hour's drive, we reached the Upi Municipal Hall, where two staff members of the Municipal Local Government Operations Officer (MLGOO) joined us. They would accompany us to the far-flung barangay of Bungcog. Another 30 minutes of rugged travel brought us to our destination, where the barangay chairperson and officials greeted us warmly.

"Welcome, welcome! Please join us for merienda," said the chairperson, her smile wide and genuine. Although we had already eaten, the spread of local delicacies was irresistible, and we graciously accepted their hospitality, treating it as a second breakfast.

STORY 4

Once refreshed, we were ushered into the Lupon Hall. Inside, the Lupon members—local dispute settlers—had been waiting for over an hour. Their anxious faces quickly transformed into smiles as we took our seats.

The Barangay Local Government Unit (BLGU) of Bungcog, like many in the uplands, is home to a predominantly Indigenous Peoples (IP) community. The Lupon in Bungcog had something remarkable to show us—their traditional methods of dispute resolution, deeply rooted in the Teduray culture.

"Let me introduce you to one of our key methods," the lady Lupon member began. "This is the Mékétéfu Sébéy, or the sacred room."

She explained that before any conflict resolution begins, both parties enter this sacred space to pray. "It doesn't matter if you are Teduray, Moro, or Christian. There's an altar for each faith—each containing a Bible or Qur'an. First, the complainant prays, then the respondent. Divine intervention, we believe, helps calm tempers."

Nods of agreement passed through the room. I could see how much these traditions were revered, binding the community in a shared belief system.

The lady continued, "Then there's the samféton—elders from each purok tasked with settling minor disputes before they even reach us."

"And these elders, are they always men?" I asked.

She smiled. "Not at all. Women can serve as samféton too. It's about respect and wisdom, not gender."

As she spoke, I realized just how progressive and inclusive their system was. It prevented the Barangay Council from becoming overwhelmed with disputes, keeping peace at the community level.

Then, we came to the more symbolic rituals. The Sékétas Déméluwas—a sacred vow between opposing parties to end their conflict—was especially fascinating. The opposing parties each held one end of a *gito*, a native weaving material. "By cutting the *gito*, the conflict ends," she explained. "Breaking the vow will bring misfortune."

"Would you mind explaining this in Teduray?" I asked, curious to hear the ritual in its original language.

As she spoke in the rich tones of Teduray, I couldn't help but notice several words that sounded familiar. "Wait, did you just say *makat'pu* (anything deemed sacred, with the belief that violating its sanctity may shorten one's life)? That's the same in Maguindanaon and Iranun!" I interjected, much to the delight of the group. Even the chairwoman was surprised at how closely related our languages were, a small but meaningful reminder of the common ground between our communities.

We also discussed the *Onuk Manok*, a particularly touching ritual. The lady Lupon member picked up a chicken egg and held it out before us. "This egg," she began, "is fragile, just like our relationships. We must handle it with care, or it will break."

I marveled at how these indigenous rituals incorporated everyday objects, like a simple egg, to convey profound messages about relationships and conflict. "This deserves a video documentary someday," I whispered to a colleague. He nodded in agreement.

Time flew by, and soon we were wrapping up. Though the chairperson insisted we stay for lunch, we had to politely decline. "We have to visit Barangay Rempes next," I explained.

"But next time, please, stay longer!" she said, half-jokingly but with genuine warmth.

"We'll make sure of it," I replied, smiling, as we waved our goodbyes.

As we drove down the winding roads toward Barangay Rempes, the words of the Lupon member echoed in my mind.

In a world where disputes can tear communities apart, these ancient rituals were living testaments to the strength of indigenous wisdom. Teduray, Moro, Christian—it didn't matter.

What mattered was the shared humanity beneath it all, fragile as an egg, yet resilient enough to be mended with care.

And in that unity, I found hope for the future.

THE TRI-JUSTICE SYSTEM IN ACTION: MY PERSONAL JOURNEY THROUGH LEGAL PLURALISM IN 15 BARMM BARANGAYS

*****

Chapter 5
THE TREE OF LIFE AND PEACE IN REMPES

The sun was high as we bounced along the narrow road leading from the remote barangay of Bungcog to Barangay Rempes, tucked deep in the mountains of Upi in Maguindanao del Norte.

The 30-minute drive was a mix of anticipation and curiosity, my thoughts occupied by yet another unique culture and practices that awaited us in this small yet vibrant community. "How do you pronounce 'Rempes' again?" I asked my companions, two local staff members from the Municipal Local Government Operations Office (MLGOO). I had a hunch that the spelling didn't match how the name was spoken. "It's 'Remp's,'" one of them replied with a knowing smile. "That's how the locals say it."

By the time we arrived at the barangay hall, it was noon, and the air was thick with the warmth of midday. Inside, the barangay secretary was still busy assisting a resident who appeared to be requesting some documents. I noticed two young boys, Fahmi and Sa'id, fidgeting at their mother's feet, clearly bored by the wait.

I knelt down to their level and smiled, "Hey, do you want to see some magic?"

Their eyes lit up, and soon I was pretending to pull a coin from the back of my neck, then magically producing it from my mouth. Fahmi clapped his hands in amazement. "How did you do that?!" he exclaimed. "It's magic," I said with a wink, as his younger brother giggled in delight.

A short while after being served lunch, we were invited into the Lupon Hall, where the real purpose of our visit would unfold. The Lupong Tagapamayapa of Barangay Rempes was about to demonstrate how they resolved disputes using techniques that honored the cultural diversity of Upi's tri-people—Christian settlers, Moro, and the Teduray tribe.

One of the first methods they showcased was the FÊLANATAN FËDAW ritual. The Lupon Chairman, serving as the mediator, explained the significance as he placed a plant in the center of the room. "This plant," he said solemnly, "represents life and peace. And now, each party will drink water." He handed glasses of water to both the complainant and the respondent. "Water brings calmness. It washes away bad intentions," he added, as both parties sipped. The symbolism was palpable, and I could feel the tension in the room begin to ease, as though the simple act of drinking water could indeed bring peace.

Next, we learned about the Timuay Justice System, an indigenous approach to resolving conflicts within the Teduray tribe. "Our tribe has always respected the wisdom of our elders, the KÊFËDUWAN," the Chairman explained. "They help mediate disputes using our customary laws, called UKIT TIGODON. We are now working to codify these laws into municipal ordinances, but for now, they continue to guide us in our quest for justice."

Curious, I asked, "What about the Moro and Christian settlers? How do they fit into this process?"

The Chairman nodded thoughtfully. "Their tribal leaders or elders join the discussions when necessary, ensuring that their beliefs and customs are also respected. We believe in a justice system that considers everyone's traditions."

As the session progressed, we witnessed the FELEGENEY FEDAW in action—a break taken when parties couldn't reach an agreement. "Let's pause," the Chairman suggested gently. "Each side will take a few minutes to reflect." Lupon members quietly approached each party, whispering advice and potential solutions. After 10 minutes, the parties returned, calmer, more willing to negotiate. It was a simple yet powerful method, a pause that allowed emotions to settle and clearer decisions to emerge.

Just as the discussions grew more intense, our team leader signaled that it was time for us to leave. I glanced back at the Lupon Hall, now filled with the soft murmur of ongoing negotiations. These practices, rooted in tradition yet adaptable to modern needs, had left a lasting impression on me.

The two staff members graciously invited us to stop by "Mhuk-Bang Food Hub" to try their signature pancit, fried chicken, and sandwiches, despite the fact that we had been well-fed throughout the day.

Afterward, I politely explained that I needed to return to Cotabato City early, so my family could attend the burial procession in Talayan of our elder cousin, an MILF commander, who had passed away earlier that day.

As we drove away from Barangay Rempes, the mountain air felt lighter, as if the weight of conflict and tension had been momentarily lifted by the profound rituals we had just witnessed. The road stretched ahead, winding back to a world that often sought swift resolutions through rules and courts, but here, in this hidden corner of Maguindanao del Norte, peace was nurtured differently—through understanding, respect, and a deep reverence for life.

I realized then that in places like Rempes, justice wasn't merely about settling disputes; it was about sustaining the delicate balance that held the community's heart together, one ritual, one conversation, one sip of water at a time.

*****

Story 6

MORIATAO LOKSADATU'S 4K'S OF SETTLEMENT

"Four hours on the road, and it felt like stepping into a different yet familiar world." That was the thought that crossed my mind as we crossed the boundary into Lanao del Sur.

After visiting several barangays in Maguindanao del Norte and del Sur, our team was now *en route* to Marawi City. The morning sun had barely risen when we left Cotabato City, and the long stretch of road ahead was a reminder of both the distance and the responsibility that lay before us.

As we arrived in Marawi City, our first stop was the Ministry of the Interior and Local Government (MILG) Provincial Office for a courtesy visit. I stepped out of the van, expecting formalities, but instead, I was greeted with a pleasant surprise.

"Sir! Sir! *As-salāmu 'alaykum!*" I turned around and saw three familiar faces beaming at me. "It's us, your former students!" There stood three of my former students from Mindanao State University, two of them now Local Government Operations Officers (LGOOs).

"Well, look at you all!" I said, shaking the hands of one of them warmly. "Seems like you're doing great things, *al-hamdulillāh!*"

They chuckled, one of them replying, "Thanks to you, sir. But now, it's our turn to welcome you!"

After some refreshments that they graciously prepared, our team was joined by two of my former students and two other provincial staff members. Together, we set off to our next destination: Barangay Moriatao Loksadatu, an hour away in the town of Taraka.

As we passed through what was once Marawi's bustling business district, I couldn't help but ask the driver, "Datu Jun, could you slow down for a moment?"

I wanted to take in the sights, or rather, the remnants of what had once been. The scars left by the 2017 Marawi Siege were still raw, buildings half-standing, as though the city itself was holding its breath. It was my first time back since the siege, and as we drove through the devastated area, I could almost hear the echoes of a city once full of life — now a silent witness to terror and 'the war on terror'.

"I can imagine the cries," I muttered softly. "The fear. The destruction. It's as if it all happened yesterday."

My reverie was interrupted when we arrived at the barangay hall in Moriatao Luksadatu. The barangay chairwoman, along with her husband, who I soon learned was the former chairman, greeted us with smiles and the unmistakable hospitality of the Maranao people.

"Welcome, *bulos kano*!" the chairwoman said as she gestured for us to partake in native delicacies they had prepared. "Please, have some food before we begin."

After we ate, we were led into the Lupon Hall, where the members of the Lupong Tagapamayapa were waiting for us. I was eager to observe the Katarungang Pambarangay in action, particularly how they employed alternative dispute resolution methods to maintain peace in their community.

One of my former students leaned over and explained, "Sir, the process here is unique. We involve traditional leaders in the mediation, and they use a combination of customary law and modern methods."

"And it works?" I asked.

"Always," he replied with confidence. "We have a 100% settlement rate."

As the mediation session begins, the Lupon Chairperson would outline the objectives of the process. "Before we start," she would address the parties, "remember that we follow the wisdom of our ancestors— *Kapamagongowa* (consultation), *Kapamagadata* (mutual respect), *Kasisiyapa* (mutual care), and *Kanggiginawai* (mutual love). These are the values that will guide us today."

The two parties would present their sides, and I could imagine the depth of respect each would show. There would be no shouting, no interruption. Instead, the Chairperson would remind them of the old Maranao saying: "We are not here to win or lose, but to find peace."

As the dialogue would continue, it would become clear how integral these traditional values are to resolving conflicts. The final step in the process would be the *KANDURI*, a celebratory feast marking the reconciliation of the parties. This celebration includes the "*panolak-o mga sapal samaya*" (nullification of the oath/vow), a traditional practice believed to negate the harmful effects of any negative words exchanged during the confrontation. As they shared food and exchanged smiles, it was as if the conflict had never existed.

"This is how we heal," the former Chairman said, turning to me with a smile. "Not just with words, but with community."

As we wrapped up, my curiosity deepened. "Tell me," I asked the former Chairman, "how does *IGHMA AGO TARIBIT*—your customary law—fit into all of this? It seems so intertwined with your approach."

He nodded. "It's the backbone. Without it, there would be no harmony. It is our guide in both legal and moral matters. In fact, the four principles are an integral part of it."

I wanted to stay longer, to learn more about the intricate ways these traditional laws shaped the lives of the people. But just as I was preparing to dive deeper into conversation, one of the provincial staff members tapped me on the shoulder. "Sir, we need to head back to Marawi. The weather's turning bad."

Looking up, I saw dark clouds forming above

the nearby hills. Fog and rain were creeping in, as they often do in this part of Lanao del Sur. Reluctantly, we said our goodbyes.

As we drove back to Marawi, I found myself lost in thought. The resilience of the Maranao people, the power of their traditions, and the enduring spirit of communities like Moriatao Loksadatu left a lasting impression on me.

In a world where conflict often leads to division, here was a place where ancient wisdom still guided the way to peace.

And perhaps, in that, there is a lesson for us all.

*****

Story 7

RANTIAN'S TAPESTRY OF TRADITION, FAITH, AND GOVERNANCE

As the sun rose over Marawi, casting golden rays across Lake Lanao, our team prepared for a journey—not just to another barangay, but into the heart of a community where tradition, faith, and modern governance intertwined to resolve conflicts.

After breakfast at the hotel, we quickly set off for Barangay Rantian in Ditsaan Ramain, just a 30-minute

THE TRI-JUSTICE SYSTEM IN ACTION: MY PERSONAL JOURNEY THROUGH LEGAL PLURALISM IN 15 BARMM BARANGAYS

drive from Marawi City. Known as the hometown of the late Senator Domocao Alonto, the founder of Mindanao State University (MSU), Ditsaan Ramain promised a blend of history and tradition, and we were eager to explore.

This time, we were accompanied by two significant figures—the Municipal Local Government Operations Officer (MLGOO) and a staff member from the Ministry of the Interior and Local Government (MILG) Provincial Office. Their presence signaled that this was not just a routine visit, but a meaningful engagement.

As we arrived, the first thing that struck us was the landscape—Rantian is lowland, long and rectangular, sitting directly beside Lake Lanao. The barangay hall, nestled near the water, stood proud, its two-story structure newly inaugurated. The young barangay chairman, his father (a retired government official), and his elder brother, who I later learned is the municipal assessor or so, together with the rest of the barangay officials, all greeted us warmly. Their hospitality was evident from the moment we stepped out of the vehicle.

The chairman, with a sense of pride, pointed to the building. "We built this hall after winning a barangay award for our community efforts," he said, his voice tinged with both accomplishment and humility.

After enjoying Maranao delicacies, we were ushered to another room on the second floor. There, the Lupong Tagapamayapa members were waiting anxiously for us. Their eagerness spoke volumes about their dedication to their role. As we settled in, I started with my usual opening remarks, assuring them that the upcoming BARMM Barangay Justice System Training Manual would not be written solely by me. "The real authors," I smiled, "are you—the ones who have been settling local disputes for years."

The young chairman and the Lupon members then began to explain the processes they use for resolving conflicts in their community. Their passion was conspicuous as they described six key techniques:

1. Monetary Assistance from the Lupon Chairman

"Sometimes," the chairman began, "financial troubles are at the root of a conflict. Offering some monetary help can calm the situation." His tone was matter-of-fact, but the gravity of the gesture was not lost on us. This financial assistance, often coming from his own pocket, acts as a bridge between the disputing parties, allowing them to find common ground.

2. Traditional/Indigenous Mechanisms (*IGHMA* and *TARITIB*)

"We still honor our tribal roots," one Lupon member added. "*TARITIB* is our customary law, and *IGHMA* brings our elders together to resolve disputes." These practices have been passed down for generations, and their relevance in today's world is still as strong as ever. By integrating these mechanisms, they ensure that every resolution is culturally rooted and respected by the community.

3. Shari'ah or Islamic Mechanism

In a community where Islam is deeply ingrained, the application of Shari'ah law is paramount. "When the dispute involves Muslim parties, we always refer to Shari'ah," the chairman said. This approach ensures that resolutions are aligned with Islamic principles, such as conciliation, forgiveness, and justice, making the process sacred and fair for all involved.

4. *KANDORI* (Through Food or Monetary Gifts)

A smile spread across the chairman's face as he explained *KANDORI*. "We believe in healing through sharing. A meal or a small gift can do wonders in breaking down barriers." The simple act of sharing food often softens hearts, and this practice reinforces the community's belief in togetherness.

5. Collective Mediation

"We never mediate alone," another Lupon member chimed in. "By involving more of us, we bring more perspectives to the table." This collective approach not only lends authority to the process but also ensures that no party feels overlooked. The added voices provide a wider range of solutions, making it harder for the disputants to refuse an amicable settlement.

6. Coordination with Relevant Agencies

STORY 7

"When needed, we call in help from other agencies," the MLGOO added. "Sometimes, a dispute involves legal or social issues beyond our scope." By working with external institutions, the Lupon ensures that every aspect of the conflict is addressed, even if it requires legal or financial interventions. This collaboration strengthens the community's ability to maintain peace long-term.

As the Lupon members continued to share their stories, I felt a growing curiosity about how these ancient traditions blended so seamlessly with modern governance. But, just as I was about to dive deeper into the discussion, the MILG staff member gently tapped my shoulder. "Sir, it's 10:31," he whispered. "We were supposed to have wrapped up 30 minutes ago, and with a long journey ahead back to Cotabato, you couldn't afford any delays."

Before we left, however, our gracious hosts insisted we stay for an early lunch. "Please, you must try our pagana Maranao," the chairman urged, referring to the Maranao banquet. The spread was too inviting to refuse, and our team gratefully obliged, savoring every bite.

As we ate, I couldn't help but think about my alma mater, Mindanao State University. I was looking forward to revisiting the campus on our way back to Cotabato City and maybe indulging in some of the famous *tapay* (fermented) ice cream. But just as I let my imagination wander, our team leader's voice snapped me back to reality. "Sir, change of plans. We need to reach the MILG Regional Office before 5 PM. No time for detours (toward MSU and the second district of the province)."

With a sigh, I whispered to myself, "See you next time, *dakilang paaralan* (great school), *in sha' Allah*."

As we drove away from Barangay Rantian along the provincial first district highway around the lake, the weight of what I had witnessed settled in. This small, lake-bound community was a beacon of how tradition, faith, and cooperation could guide a modern world toward peace. It wasn't just about resolving conflicts—it was about preserving the delicate fabric of unity.

In that moment, I realized: peace isn't just the absence of conflict. It's an ever-present commitment to understanding, respect, and shared responsibility.

*****

Story 8

POBLACION VII'S SILT ISLAND OF TRI-JUSTICE SYSTEM

While waiting for the schedule of our flight to the island provinces of Tawi-Tawi, Sulu, and Basilan, our team had to visit a barangay in Cotabato City and another in the Special Geographic Area (SGA).

After lunch, we set off for Poblacion VII, a vibrant part of the city located on the *Tuka na Nan's* river island. This neighborhood has an intriguing history.

THE TRI-JUSTICE SYSTEM IN ACTION: MY PERSONAL JOURNEY THROUGH LEGAL PLURALISM IN 15 BARMM BARANGAYS

Back in September 1960, heavy rains caused severe flooding, worsened by the silting of the Pulangi River bed. The floodwaters rose waist-deep in the downtown area. In response, then Congressman Salipada Pendatun coordinated with the national government to send dredgers to create a cut-off channel, forming what is now the silt island of which Poblacion VII is a part. Technically, the island is still part of the river and considered public property. This explains the barangay's dense population, a melting pot of Moro (Maguindanaon and Iranun), Christian settlers, and Non-Moro Indigenous Peoples (NMIP).

The narrow roads of the barangay barely allowed for two-way traffic, and as we approached the barangay hall, we were greeted by the eager faces of the Lupon Tagapamayapa members, who were already waiting for us. The barangay secretary and the deputy Lupon leader greeted us with warm smiles, apologizing on behalf of the chairman who was attending a meeting at the city hall.

Once seated, our team leader opened the session by explaining the purpose of our visit. I followed with my usual icebreaker. "I'm not here to write the barangay justice system manual," I said with a smile, "You all are the experts. You've been handling disputes for years. So really, you'll be writing this with your experiences."

At first, the conversation was slow to pick up, with only the Lupon leader and the barangay secretary chiming in as one member hesitantly suggested earlier, "Maybe only the selected Lupon members should speak?"

But I encouraged everyone to share their thoughts. "We want to hear from as many of you as possible. Every perspective is valuable."

With that, almost every Lupon member began contributing, turning the session into a lively exchange of ideas. Despite the refreshments they had generously provided, no one paused the discussion. It was clear that they had much to say.

I was fascinated by the depth of their insights. The Lupong Tagapamayapa, or the Barangay Justice System, employs an array of methods to resolve conflicts and maintain peace. One key strategy is crafting localized resolutions tailored to amicably settle disputes. These resolutions ensure fairness and are widely accepted by the community.

"We don't just rely on policies," explained one elder. "We also involve the council of elders and tribal leaders. Their wisdom and understanding of local customs help guide the mediation."

Another member nodded in agreement. "Yes, their role is crucial. When they step in, it's not just about the law. It's about respecting traditions and keeping the peace."

I was struck by how their system blends the legal, cultural, and spiritual. They don't just resolve conflicts through secular means—spiritual guidance is also part of the process, especially when tensions run high. The council often invokes religious teachings to encourage forgiveness and reconciliation.

"Our faith plays a big part," one Lupon member added thoughtfully. "We remind people that peace and forgiveness are values that go beyond just resolving a dispute."

The diversity of Poblacion VII is reflected in its justice system. The Lupon members themselves represent the multicultural makeup of the barangay, including Moro, Christian settlers, and NMIP. This diversity is not just symbolic—it's vital. Their justice system is a tri-justice system, one that mirrors the community's tri-people composition.

"When we handle disputes," one Lupon member explained, "we make sure that the customs of the Moro, Christian settlers, and NMIP are respected equally. It's not easy, but it's necessary."

By incorporating the perspectives of all three groups, the barangay has built a more inclusive and effective justice system. Given that the majority of the population is Moro, the system naturally accommodates their customs, but it never neglects the rights and traditions of the Christian settlers and NMIP.

As the discussion deepened, I lost track of time, fully immersed in their stories of conflict resolution. It wasn't until our team leader gently tapped my shoulder and whispered, "It's late. We need to wrap up," that I realized it's almost five in the afternoon.

This tri-justice system, with its blend of legal, cultural, and spiritual frameworks, fosters a harmonious community where conflicts are resolved with respect for each group's identity. By accommodating diverse beliefs and traditions, the barangay has created not just a justice system, but a culture of peace.

As we packed up to leave, I couldn't help but think that if more communities embraced this kind of approach—where justice is shaped by understanding and respect for diversity—the world would be a much more peaceful place.

*****

Story 9

TUMBRAS' SEEDS OF JUSTICE AND HARMONY

Sometimes, a journey is more than just a destination; it's a window into a community's soul.

After a hearty breakfast, our team set off from Cotabato City, bound for Barangay Tumbras, huddled in the newly formed Kadayangan Municipality within the BARMM Special Geographic Area (SGA).

THE TRI-JUSTICE SYSTEM IN ACTION: MY PERSONAL JOURNEY THROUGH LEGAL PLURALISM IN 15 BARMM BARANGAYS

Our mission was to engage with the Lupon Tagapamayapa members and learn about their community-based justice system. However, as often happens in the field, a miscommunication delayed our plans. It seemed our visit had been mistakenly believed to be postponed, leaving us with an unexpected hour of waiting while the barangay secretary gathered the Lupon members.

Once the team assembled and we had enjoyed the warm hospitality of a shared lunch, we were ready to begin. I opened our focused group discussion with my usual disclaimer. "Let me make one thing clear," I began, smiling at the attentive faces around me. "This training manual we're discussing—I'm not its author. You are. You're the experts on dispute resolution in this barangay. I'm just here to serve as your 'secretary.'" This approach always sets the tone for a collaborative, open dialogue.

As the conversation unfolded, I was introduced to a fascinating practice that highlights the barangay's unique approach to conflict resolution: the KP Peace Cage. "If tempers flare during mediation," one Lupon member explained, "we call for a coffee break. One party is invited to step into the Peace Cage." Intrigued, I asked, "What exactly happens in the Peace Cage?"

The member smiled. "It's not as ominous as it sounds," he clarified. "The Peace Cage is simply a quiet space where the party can calm down with a cup of coffee, and one of us talks to them. We guide them through their emotions and help them reflect. After 10 or 20 minutes, we resume mediation in a calmer, more productive manner."

But what truly captured my attention was the symbolic gesture at the end of each resolved case. "After settling the dispute," another member shared, "the parties plant a coconut tree together. We call it 'Puno ng Buhay,' the Tree of Life. It's a living reminder of their commitment to peace." This ritual, I thought, beautifully encapsulates the spirit of resolution—planting seeds of harmony where conflict once thrived.

As the discussion deepened, it became evident that Barangay Tumbras' Lupon members were a reflection of the community's rich diversity. "Our Lupon mirrors the barangay itself," a local elder noted. "We have both Moro, specifically Iranun and Maguindanaon, and Christian settlers represented here." This balance, he explained, is crucial to ensuring that the various cultural and religious backgrounds of the community are respected and considered in every conflict resolution.

The demographic majority of Barangay Tumbras is Moro Iranun and Maguindanaon, whose traditional methods of dispute settlement heavily influence the Lupon's processes. These methods, deeply rooted in collective decision-making and reconciliation, focus on restoring relationships rather than simply punishing wrongdoers. "It's not just about settling a dispute," said one of the Lupon leaders. "It's about healing the community."

I learned that the Lupon often incorporates Moro Maguindanaon customary laws, which draw on centuries-old traditions of mediation facilitated by respected elders or religious leaders. "Our process respects both Islamic principles and local customs," one Lupon mediator explained. "We aim for a resolution that feels fair to everyone involved."

Yet, the inclusion of Christian settlers within the Lupon ensures that the voices of this minority are also heard. "While our methods may be rooted in Moro traditions," the barangay secretary pointed out, "we make sure to include Christian perspectives. Our goal is peace across the entire community, not just within one group."

This inclusive approach, I realized, is a testament to the barangay's commitment to unity and coexistence in a multicultural setting.

As the clock edged past 3 p.m., we reluctantly wrapped up the discussion. I could sense that we had only scratched the surface of the rich knowledge and wisdom this barangay had to offer. Still, the afternoon had given me a deep appreciation of how culture, tradition, and community values shape their justice system.

On our way back to Cotabato City, we stopped briefly in the town of Pigcayawan for a refreshing glass of buko juice. Under the heat of the midday sun, I couldn't help but reflect on the profound significance of Barangay Tumbras' tri-justice system.

In this newly formed town, born from Midsayap, the seeds of a more inclusive and harmonious future are being carefully planted—just like the coconut trees in the 'Puno ng Buhay' ritual.

As we resumed our journey, I felt a quiet optimism. If every community could nurture justice like they nurture life, perhaps there's hope for peace in every corner of the world.

*****

Story 10

LAMION'S PATHWAY TO COMMUNITY HARMONY

After an intense 10-day marathon of visiting nine barangays on the mainland of BARMM, it was finally time to explore the region's three island provinces.

THE TRI-JUSTICE SYSTEM IN ACTION: MY PERSONAL JOURNEY THROUGH LEGAL PLURALISM IN 15 BARMM BARANGAYS

At Cotabato Airport, I met our energetic young team leader, and soon, we were off on an early morning flight to Bongao, Tawi-Tawi. The weather was perfect, and the flight went smoothly. Upon landing, the Ministry of the Interior and Local Government (MILG) Provincial Office greeted us warmly. A solid delegation of four had been sent to accompany us on our barangay visits. Sir Cid, the delegates head, conveyed the Provincial Director's apologies for not being able to join us, as he was attending an official event in Davao City.

As we made our way to the town center, I took in the breathtaking coastal views of Bongao, with the imposing Bud Bongao standing like a sentinel, watching over the island for centuries. After an early check-in at Rachel's Hotel, I discovered that our first barangay, Lamion, was conveniently located just a short walk away. We decided to take the 10-minute stroll, enjoying the island atmosphere.

Lamion, being in the heart of Bongao, is a vibrant community made up of various cultural groups, including Moro (Tausug and Sama), settlers, and the Indigenous Peoples (IPs) known as Badjao. This diversity creates a dynamic social fabric, and the Barangay Hall is strategically positioned near Datu Halun Sakilan Memorial Hospital, making it easier to address disputes, especially those involving physical injuries, with immediate access to medical care—facilitating quicker, more effective resolutions.

STORY 10

Upon arrival, we were warmly welcomed by the young barangay chairman and the seasoned barangay secretary. The focus group discussion (FGD) included two female members of the Lupon. I began by stressing that the training manual being developed for the MILG wouldn't be authored by me, but by the Lupon members themselves, who bring years of valuable experience in resolving disputes and employing various techniques across BARMM's diverse communities.

During our deep and insightful conversation, the members of the Lupong Tagapamayapa shared some of their unique approaches to conflict resolution, shaped by the cultural mix of Lamion:

"Our process begins with a Pre-Mediation Conference," the young barangay chairman explained. "This allows both parties to air their concerns before formal mediation starts. It sets a positive tone and gives everyone a chance to share their perspective early on."

The barangay secretary added, "We also provide Religious Guidance for those involved, whether they are Muslim or Christian. We tailor this counsel to their beliefs, helping them find common ground based on shared values of respect and reconciliation."

One of the female Lupon members shared another key practice: "Many people can't participate fully because of financial difficulties. So, we offer Financial Assistance, covering transportation, food, or even medical expenses. It ensures that no one is excluded from the mediation process due to lack of resources."

Another member mentioned their Government Agency Help Lines, saying, "We maintain direct communication with government agencies to give quick advice when needed. Whether it's legal guidance or social services, we can access the support necessary to aid the resolution process."

"And after mediation," the chairman continued, "we don't just end things there. We organize Bonding and Reconnection Activities to help the parties rebuild trust. These could be community events or shared meals, which play a vital role in healing relationships and restoring a sense of unity."

These innovative techniques reflect the Lupong Tagapamayapa's deep commitment to resolving disputes in a way that's fair, compassionate, and culturally sensitive to the diverse groups in Lamion. Their methods go beyond resolving immediate issues—they focus on healing, reconciliation, and fostering lasting peace in a multi-ethnic community.

After the FGD, the team generously offered us snacks and invited us to stay for lunch. Unfortunately, due to our tight schedule and the need to visit another barangay during lunch hour, we had to decline.

The visit to Barangay Lamion revealed more than just effective dispute resolution methods—it illuminated the deep resilience and unity of a diverse community committed to lasting peace. Through their culturally grounded and innovative practices, they are shaping a future where conflicts are not just settled but transformed into opportunities for growth and reconciliation.

*****

Story 11
TUBIG-BOH'S CONFLICT RESOLUTION WITH HEART

The sun was already high when we left Barangay Lamion, our spirits buoyed by the warm Tawi-Tawi air, heading for our next stop.

THE TRI-JUSTICE SYSTEM IN ACTION: MY PERSONAL JOURNEY THROUGH LEGAL PLURALISM IN 15 BARMM BARANGAYS

From Barangay Lamion, located on the northeastern part of Bongao Island, our team set out for Barangay Tubig-Boh, nestled in the southeastern part of Tawi-Tawi's provincial capital. The drive took just about 10 minutes, even in the late morning bustle. As we arrived, we were greeted warmly by the acting barangay secretary, Lupon members, and other local officials since the barangay chairwoman was on official leave.

The first thing that caught my attention was the layout of their community spaces. Their medical clinic was seamlessly integrated into the Lupong Tagapamayapa Hall, allowing immediate medical treatment to play a pivotal role in resolving disputes, particularly when minor physical injuries were involved. It struck me how this practical design enhanced their ability to mediate conflicts on the spot, ensuring that health needs were addressed as part of the overall process.

As we gathered inside, I made my usual introduction, explaining that I wasn't here to author the Barangay Justice System Training Manual but to be their scribe. "The real authors," I told them, "are none other than yourselves." This seemed to resonate, and soon, the Lupon members were enthusiastically sharing their insights and experiences with me.

"We focus on the whole person," one of the Lupon members said. "We don't just look at the problem, we look at the people involved—how they're feeling and what they need." This holistic approach was evident in their innovative settlement techniques, which they eagerly outlined for me:

1. Psychological and Medical First Aid: "When people come to us with a dispute," the barangay secretary explained, "we make sure they're well, both in mind and body. It's hard to resolve anything when you're hurt or upset." By offering immediate psychological and medical support, the council ensures that disputing parties are in a stable condition, ready to engage meaningfully in mediation. This approach underscores the belief that mental and physical health are essential to reaching a fair and lasting resolution.

2. Financial Assistance for Both Parties: "Sometimes, the obstacle to justice isn't the conflict itself but the costs involved," a Lupon member noted. To address this, Barangay Tubig-Boh provides financial assistance, covering expenses such as fines for elopement, transportation, and even medical costs. "We want to level the playing field," he added, "so no one feels they're at a disadvantage because of money."

3. Government Agency Help Lines: The barangay has also established dedicated helplines, directly linking individuals to various government agencies for legal advice and guidance. "We don't have all the answers, but we know who does," another member said with a smile, emphasizing how these connections help disputants make informed decisions during mediation.

4. Logistical Support from the Ministry of the Interior and Local Government (MILG): The barangay receives logistical assistance from the MILG, enabling them to manage conflicts more efficiently. "We couldn't do what we do without their support," the secretary said, referring to the transportation, communication tools, and other resources provided by the ministry.

5. Coordination with Other Agencies: "We're never working alone," the barangay secretary stressed. The Lupon actively coordinates with various government and non-government agencies, ensuring that a wide array of resources is available to address the needs of all parties involved. This collaboration ensures that no stone is left unturned in their pursuit of justice.

It became clear that the Lupong Tagapamayapa of Barangay Tubig-Boh is deeply committed to creating a just and equitable process for resolving disputes. Their approach is not just about resolving the present conflict but ensuring the well-being of everyone involved, making sure they have the resources they need to move forward.

As I grew more fascinated with these techniques, the barangay secretary interrupted our discussion with a gentle reminder: "It's past noon already. We've prepared lunch for you—fresh seafood, mostly." We were led to a modest spread, a meal prepared with the same care and hospitality they extended throughout our visit.

On the drive back to Rachel's Hotel, I couldn't help but reflect on the depth of what I had witnessed. The island provinces, with their unique blend of cultures and challenges, had given me my first taste of conflict resolution that truly understood the human heart—and that, I realized, was the key to its success.

*****

Story 12
WALKING AROUND LIKE A NATIVE OF BONGAO

After resting sufficiently from my visits to two barangays, I decided to take a leisurely late-afternoon walk, blending in like a native around the streets near Rachel's Hotel. This has become a personal ritual whenever I'm in a new place—walking around as if I belong.

Starting from Tubig Mampallam Road, where the hotel is located, I wandered along both sides of Lamiyon Road before circling back to Mampallam Road and heading towards Ridjiki Boulevard. There, I came across the Tabuh Bongao Public Market. Like a local, I resisted the urge to take photos while inside the market, immersing myself fully in the experience.

As I made my way back to the hotel after about 15 minutes of walking, the serene sound of the Muslim call to prayer (*adhān*) began to echo from the nearby masjids, perfectly accompanying my evening snack of fresh durian and mangosteen an hour after dinner.

***

STORY 12

CONQUERING BUD BONGAO

No visit to the provincial capital of Tawi-Tawi would be complete without a trek up Bud Bongao, the iconic peak of Bongao.

THE TRI-JUSTICE SYSTEM IN ACTION: MY PERSONAL JOURNEY THROUGH LEGAL PLURALISM IN 15 BARMM BARANGAYS

Before you begin the climb, your first stop should be at a nearby store to buy some bananas. These will come in handy for feeding the friendly monkeys that greet you along the trail. After that, don't forget to grab your admission ticket at the designated tourism office.

Now, you might be wondering, "Did you make it to the top?"

Next question, please!

***

A MUST CAMPUS TOUR

Of course, campus tour – though just a quick one – to Tawi-Tawi's "dakilang paaralan, Pamantasang

STORY 12

Mindanao" (Mindanao State University – Tawi-Tawi Campus) is a MUST.

*****

Story 13

SULU MYSTERIES OF A PROUD PAST

"Are we going to make it?" I muttered to myself, watching the time tick away.

THE TRI-JUSTICE SYSTEM IN ACTION: MY PERSONAL JOURNEY THROUGH LEGAL PLURALISM IN 15 BARMM BARANGAYS

After an overnight stay and a visit to two barangays in Bongao, Tawi-Tawi, we were racing against the clock. Our next destination? Zamboanga City, where we needed to catch a ferry to Sulu by early evening. But the day had other plans. Our 4 PM flight was delayed by an hour, and with each passing minute, the uncertainty of catching the ferry grew heavier.

As soon as we landed, the adrenaline surged. We had no choice but to submit to the whims of the taxi driver who charged us Php500 for a rushed trip from the airport to the pier. Upon arrival, MV Aleson Ferry 1 was just about to close its gates. Breathless, we flashed our tickets at the guard. "We made it!" my team leader from the Ministry of the Interior and Local Government (MILG) Regional Office whispered, more to ourselves than anyone else.

The sea was merciful that night, or perhaps we were too exhausted to notice anything but our deep slumber. Either way, the smooth overnight travel carried us closer to our destination.

"Lebol, lebol!" shouted the young men as they boarded the ferry early in the morning. Their calls offering to carry passengers' baggage woke me. "We're here," I thought, realizing we had arrived in *Lupah Sūg*, the land of the brave. As we disembarked, the same eager voices echoed, "Motol, motol!"—motorcycle services were being offered as we navigated the light drizzle.

STORY 12

Our reception at the pier was warm, despite the rain. A Municipal Local Government Operations Officer (MLGOO) and a staff member from the MILG Provincial Office were waiting to fetch us. "PD (Provincial Director) sends her regards and apologies," they explained. "She's on official travel." With that, we were whisked away to Dennis Coffee Shop along Scott Road for an early breakfast—a spread of *satti* and traditional Tausug sweet delicacies.

After the meal, we had a brief respite at the Sulu State College dormitory. Two hours of rest was all we had before heading to Talipao Municipality at exactly 8 AM. We first made a quick stop at the MILG Provincial Office, located within the Sulu Provincial Capitol compound, for a courtesy call to the Provincial Director Officer-in-Charge (OIC). As we drove through the streets, I noticed something unusual about the layout of the roads.

"Did you know that these roads are shaped like a sword?" Ma'am Jane said, pointing out the window. "If you look closely, you'll see the handle right there."

I peered out of the window, intrigued by the symbolism and the striking design. "A sword? That's an interesting choice for a road layout," I mused, imagining how the streets must have been deliberately constructed to embody the region's heroic warrior spirit.

After a quick stop to snap a picture at the iconic "I Love Sulu" sign, we passed by the Sulu National

Museum. That's when Ma'am Jane surprised me with a suggestion.

"Sir, would you like to check out the museum before we head to Talipao?" she asked, her tone light but curious, as if the idea had just struck her.

"Absolutely!" I said without hesitation, grateful for the unexpected opportunity.

The less-than-an-hour museum tour turned out to be a whirlwind journey through time, a window into the vibrant history, culture, and civilization of the "People of the Current"—the proud Tausug. Walking through the exhibits felt like traveling through centuries of rich tradition, from the grandeur of Sulu's sultanate to the region's deep-rooted cultural identity. The artifacts and displays were a testament to the wealth of natural and human resources that have shaped Sulu's story.

"It's amazing to think about how much history is packed into this small space," I remarked to museum guide as we wandered through a gallery of ancient textiles and weaponry.

"I agree," he nodded. "There's so much more to learn about this place. Every artifact here has a story."

Though I had a thousand more questions for the guide, time wasn't on our side. I longed to linger and dive deeper into Sulu's fascinating past, but our schedule demanded otherwise. By 9 AM, we were back on the road, making a quick stop at the Mindanao

STORY 12

State University (MSU) Sulu Campus—at my insistence—before continuing our journey to Talipao.

*****

Story 14

MODERN 'LANGGAL' AS BILAAN'S HEART OF PEACE

The hour-long drive from Mindanao State University (MSU) Sulu Campus allowed me to reflect not only on the region's transformation in terms of peace and order but also on Talipao's size and significance.

"Talipao has 52 barangays?" I asked Ma'am Jane, somewhat surprised.

"Yes," she confirmed. "It's a first-class municipality, one of the largest in Sulu."

This was fascinating. A municipality this large would be a prime target for gerrymandering in other provinces of the region. But here, it stood firm, its boundaries untouched by the political manipulation often seen elsewhere.

Along the way, I couldn't help but notice the visible shift in the region's security landscape. Military personnel were no longer patrolling in full battle gear, but were now engaged in civic tasks, such as cleaning the highways. This subtle transformation spoke volumes about the improved peace and order in the area.

When we arrived at Barangay Bilaan (Poblacion) Hall, the young and dynamic chairwoman and her barangay team greeted us with warmth. Following a brief introduction, we made our way to the Lupong Tagamapayapa Hall, where its members had been patiently waiting. Their eager faces lit up as we entered, but what caught my attention first was the location of the hall—situated between a grand mosque (Hadja Sitti Raya Masjid) and a two-story concrete madrasah

(Madrasah Madinat al-'Ilm). I couldn't help but share my observation with the chairwoman.

"This is more than just a strategic spot," I told her, grinning. "It reminds me of the old *langgal* or *ranggar*, where people would pray and settle disputes. It's as if the modern Lupong Tagamapayapa Hall has inherited that legacy."

Before I began the discussion, I made my usual disclaimer: "I'm not here to write your manual on the Barangay Justice System. You, with your lived experience, are the true authors."

The focus group discussion (FGD) with the Lupon members, all Tausug, was enlightening. As they shared their techniques for resolving disputes, the room filled with stories, experiences, and insights into their culturally rich mediation process.

1. Strategic Location of the Lupon Office: The office's position between the mosque and madrasah wasn't a mere coincidence. One of the Lupon members explained, "We've always believed that settling disputes here, between these two sacred institutions, brings a sense of spiritual weight to the process. The parties involved understand that this isn't just about legal resolution; it's about restoring peace in a way that aligns with our faith." This location, echoing the traditions of settling disputes in a *langgal* or mosque, symbolized the integration of faith and justice.

2. Post-Prayer Mediation: Another member chimed in, "We often schedule the mediation right after prayer. People are calmer, more reflective after they've connected with Allah. It helps them enter the discussion with an open heart." This approach ensured that the atmosphere during mediation was not only peaceful but spiritually grounded, fostering an environment conducive to reconciliation.

3. Pre-Mediation at the Sitio Level: The pre-mediation process was a vital step, as shared by the Barangay Chairperson: "Before the formal mediation, we meet with the parties in their sitio or purok. It's informal, and it allows us to hear both sides in a comfortable setting. It's like sitting with neighbors and having a talk before things get serious." This early engagement helped uncover the root causes of the dispute and prepared both parties for a more structured mediation.

4. Monetary Assistance: In cases where financial burdens could obstruct peace, the Chairperson offered a unique solution. "Sometimes, disputes involve fines or dowers, and not everyone can afford it," she said. "When needed, I step in and provide assistance. It's an old tradition—just like the datus or sultans who would help resolve conflicts with financial aid." This practice removed financial barriers that might have otherwise prolonged the conflict.

5. Shari'ah and Customary Law: One of the elders explained how Shari'ah and Moro customary laws are

often employed. "For certain cases, we use *pagsappa*—swearing on the Qur'an," he said. "It's a serious act, and people here respect it deeply. When someone swears on the Qur'an, they know they are making a commitment not just to the community, but to Allah." This blend of legal and religious traditions ensured that the resolutions carried moral weight.

6. Counseling by Elders and Religious Leaders: The role of elders and religious figures was central to the Lupon's success. "Our elders have seen it all," one of the younger Lupon members said with admiration. "They bring wisdom and experience that we don't have. And when they counsel the disputing parties, people listen." Religious leaders, too, played a key role, grounding the resolution process in both community tradition and spiritual guidance.

7. Handshake of Peace: A handshake marked the end of every mediation, a simple but powerful act. "After everything is said and done, we encourage the parties to shake hands," the Chairperson explained. "It's a gesture that signifies the end of conflict and the beginning of reconciliation. It's a small thing, but it has a big impact. It shows that both sides are willing to move forward."

These conversations with the Lupon members revealed how deeply intertwined their methods were with the community's cultural and religious values. Each technique was more than just a strategy—it was a reflection of the Tausug way of life, where faith, respect, and tradition shaped justice.

THE TRI-JUSTICE SYSTEM IN ACTION: MY PERSONAL JOURNEY THROUGH LEGAL PLURALISM IN 15 BARMM BARANGAYS

As the Lupon members shared their stories over snacks, their passion for maintaining peace was evident. Our time was limited, however, and Ma'am Jane signaled it was time to go. After a hearty lunch and a brief tour of the Municipal Hall, I learned that Talipao was a consistent recipient of the Seal of Good Local Governance—an honor that reflected the collective effort of its people.

Looking back on that day, it was clear that the community of *Lupah Sūg* had not only embraced peace but had woven it into the very fabric of their daily lives.

In the end, it's not the laws or the halls of justice that keep the peace. It's the people, their faith, and their unwavering commitment to their community.

This journey into Sulu reminded me that in the heart of every peaceful resolution lies not just a rule, but a relationship built on trust, respect, and tradition.

*****

Story 15
IF ONLY ASTANA COULD SPEAK

Every journey holds surprises, but this one was steeped in history, culture, and a hint of unexpected hospitality.

THE TRI-JUSTICE SYSTEM IN ACTION: MY PERSONAL JOURNEY THROUGH LEGAL PLURALISM IN 15 BARMM BARANGAYS

On our way back to the Sulu capital to visit another barangay, we had some stopovers and detours, each more intriguing than the last.

Our first stopover was at the Replica of Astana Darul Jambangan, perched in Mt. Bayug Eco-Cultural Park, still within the town of Talipao. This location is also home to the 1101st Infantry "Gagandilan" Brigade of the Philippine Army. The palace, whose name literally means "Palace of Abundant Flowers," was once the royal residence of the Sultanate of Sulu, a breathtaking glimpse into a bygone era of splendor.

After snapping a few photos of the majestic palace replica, we were about to leave when a young army major from Negros, approached us with a warm invitation. "You can't leave just yet," he said with a grin. "How about a cup of *Kahawa Sūg* and some dragon fruit fresh from our garden?" His offer was too tempting to refuse. So, we followed him to the camp's rooftop, where a panoramic view of the surrounding hills and distant mountains greeted us.

As we sipped the rich, earthy brew of Sulu robusta coffee, our conversation drifted naturally from topic to topic. The young major shared stories of the palace replica's construction. "It took nine months to build, back in 2013," he recounted proudly. "The brainchild of Lt. Col. Romulo Quemado II. He wanted to show that the Armed Forces appreciate the rich history of Sulu, despite it being forgotten by many."

STORY 12

I asked him what it was like back in the days when conflict gripped the province. He motioned toward the distant mountains. "See those peaks? They were Abu Sayyaf strongholds when I first arrived here. We used to launch hot-pursuit operations there. But now, we go to those same mountains with government aid – to bring livelihood projects, not bullets," he said, a sense of pride in his voice.

Our host was also eager to talk about lighter topics. "You should've seen our last marathon," he laughed. "Military men from our camp took the top spots. And not just in marathons, we've started winning triathlons, too!"

Once we finished our coffee, we said our goodbyes and resumed our journey. As we headed toward Maimbung Municipality, I couldn't help but feel a newfound respect for the soldiers not only protecting this land but nurturing it.

Our next stop was the ongoing reconstruction of the original Astana, the Sultanate's royal palace. The original palace was built in 1876 but tragically destroyed by a typhoon in 1932. Watching the workers restore what had once been a symbol of Sulu's might, I realized how much of its history was still alive, just waiting to be rediscovered.

From there, we made a detour down a narrow road leading to Tambuang Falls Resort. "The pandemic gave us the push we needed," Ma'am Jane explained. "With people unable to travel to Zamboanga City, we developed our local tourist spots." Tambuang Falls was just one of the many hidden gems they were uncovering, providing a refreshing change of pace and a boost to local tourism.

As we reached Jolo, I couldn't resist taking a photo in front of the Sulu Grand Mosque (Masjid Tulay) along Serantes Street – a stunning piece of architecture that commands attention in the heart of the city.

As our journey drew to a close and we approached our final barangay stop, I reflected on the beauty and resilience of Sulu. The Astana, both the replica and the reconstruction, stood as a powerful symbol of this province's proud heritage. What stories could the palace tell, I wondered, if only it had the voice to speak?

The roads we traveled may have wound through history and hardship, but they were also filled with hope – a tribute to a land that refuses to let its legacy be forgotten.

*****

Story 16

BUS-BUS – WHERE NEIGHBORS MEND AND PEACE ENDURES

The first thing that caught my eyes as we cruised down Serantes Road was the majestic Sulu Grand Mosque, its imposing twin towers gleaming in the

THE TRI-JUSTICE SYSTEM IN ACTION: MY PERSONAL JOURNEY THROUGH LEGAL PLURALISM IN 15 BARMM BARANGAYS

afternoon sun. What was supposed to be a quick stop for a photo soon turned into an impromptu adventure. Before we knew it, we had crossed the stretch of Taglibi Road, our destination closer than expected.

"Barangay Bus-Bus," Ma'am Jane mentioned as we drove, "is one of the most populated and economically thriving barangays in Sulu's capital. It's also a place rich with stories."

As we arrived, the barangay officials, led by their determined chairwoman, were already waiting for us at the entrance of the hall. Their smiles and warm welcome reflected the tight-knit community that thrives in this bustling part of town. As we toured the barangay hall, I couldn't help but notice the plaques and awards lining the walls—symbols of excellence, especially under the leadership of the chairwoman's husband, the former chairman.

"Our barangay is multi-awarded," she proudly shared. "It wasn't easy, but we've worked hard to maintain the standards my husband set. Our Disaster Risk Reduction Management office, for instance, is operational 24/7, always ready for emergencies."

The sense of pride in her voice was obvious. The hall buzzed with activity, and their dedication to service was evident in the equipment neatly displayed, ready to be deployed at a moment's notice.

When it was my turn to speak, I made sure to preface my remarks with my usual disclaimer. "You may have the impression that I will write the training manual," I said, "but let me be clear: you, with your years of experience, are the true authors of this barangay justice system."

As we transitioned into the focus group discussion (FGD), I could tell this was no ordinary gathering. These members of the Lupong Tagapamayapa had mediated countless disputes, and their strategies were deeply rooted in both tradition and innovation. I listened intently as they outlined their methods:

"First, we always let both parties tell their story," one of the senior Lupon members began. "It's important that they feel heard. Often, the root cause of the dispute lies deeper than what's on the surface."

Another member chimed in, "Once we understand their sides, we emphasize reconciliation. We don't want just to solve a problem—we want peace that lasts, especially for the families involved."

The chairwoman added, "In some cases, we provide financial assistance to encourage settlements. Sometimes, money is the only way to 'buy peace,' as we say."

I was particularly struck by their approach to culturally sensitive disputes. "When we mediate cases involving our Indigenous Peoples, like the Banjao," one Lupon explained, "we make sure an IP member of the Lupon is there. They know the customs and can communicate in the dialect. It's all about respect."

THE TRI-JUSTICE SYSTEM IN ACTION: MY PERSONAL JOURNEY
THROUGH LEGAL PLURALISM IN 15 BARMM BARANGAYS

Another nodded and added, "And if things get really tough, we call on respected former officials. They bring authority and experience that help calm things down."

As the discussion unfolded, I could see that they had so much more to say. I encouraged them to speak in the local *Bahasa Sūg* if it helped express their ideas more freely. And that was the key—once the floodgates opened, stories poured out like a stream. Almost every Lupon member eagerly shared case after case, often dealing with deeply personal disputes such as crimes against chastity and honor.

"This one time," one of the Lupon members recalled, "we had a case of a family feud that had lasted for years. But after hours of mediation, we managed to get them to reconcile. Now, they live peacefully side by side."

The hours flew by. It became one of the longest FGDs I'd held across the 15 barangays we had visited so far, and I could tell that this community took immense pride in their work. Their methods were not just about justice; they were about restoring harmony, ensuring that peace in Barangay Bus-Bus wasn't just a fleeting moment but a lasting way of life.

As our time together drew to a close, the chairwoman wouldn't hear of us leaving without joining them for an early dinner. "You can't leave on an empty stomach," she insisted, laughing as we graciously accepted the invitation.

STORY 12

Later that evening, back at the Sulu State College dorm, we rested for an hour before the call to Maghrib prayers echoed through the air. My teammate and I then made our way to Jolo pier, ready for the overnight journey back to Zamboanga City.

As the sea monster of a ferry rumbled to life beneath my feet, I found myself reflecting on everything I had witnessed. From Barangay Bilaan in Talipao to Barangay Bus-Bus in the capital, one thing was clear: the heart of these communities beats with resilience, solidarity, and an unwavering commitment to peace.

And as the waves lapped against the hull, I couldn't help but think—perhaps that's the greatest discovery of all.

*****

Story 17
TUMAHUBONG'S VOICES OF RESOLUTION

The sea shimmered under the moonlight as our Montenegro ferry cruised smoothly back to Zamboanga City. It felt just as peaceful as the previous

THE TRI-JUSTICE SYSTEM IN ACTION: MY PERSONAL JOURNEY THROUGH LEGAL PLURALISM IN 15 BARMM BARANGAYS

night when we traveled to Sulu—or so we thought, until we drifted into slumber, unaware of the waves that would later stir.

The following morning, we embarked on our scheduled trip to Basilan. Our brief but restful night in Zamboanga City recharged us for the day ahead.

At 8:15 a.m., the Weesam Express seacraft whisked us toward Isabela City, where we arrived in less than two hours. A delegation of Municipal Local Government Operations Officers (MLGOOs) and a staff member from the Ministry of the Interior and Local Government (MILG) Provincial Office greeted us at the port, ready to guide us through the day.

Our first stop was the MILG Provincial Office for a courtesy visit. After being offered refreshments featuring local Basilan delicacies, Ma'am Jolina conveyed a message from the Provincial Director: "She sends her warmest regards and apologizes for not being here. She's on official travel but welcomes you wholeheartedly to Basilan."

By mid-morning, we were back on the road, heading toward Sumisip Municipality. We made a quick five-minute stop at Basilan State College's Sta. Clara Campus to personally deliver two books I had recently translated—"Fiṭrah: Man's Natural Disposition" and "The Mysticism of Ḥāfiẓ" by Shahid Murtaḍā Muṭahharī. Then, we continued our journey, opting for a secondary road through Lamitan City to avoid the bustling traffic, before rejoining the national highway at Tuburan Municipality.

At around 11:30 a.m., we arrived at Tumahubong Barangay Hall. The barangay chairman and a group of Lupon members, all gathered in anticipation since the early hours of the morning, welcomed us warmly. In his speech, the chairman's voice trembled with pride, "It is an honor for our barangay to be one of the 15 chosen by the MILG Regional Office. Our community, mostly Yakan, has waited long for this moment."

Our focus group discussion (FGD) soon followed, centered on the development of a training manual for the barangay justice system. I began by setting expectations. "This manual will not be authored by me, but by you—those who have lived through countless disputes and found resolutions in ways only you can." Their experiences were profound, rooted in cultural wisdom and years of practice.

One Lupon member, a settler and brother to the two MLGOOs accompanying us, shared his methods. "We always start with a prayer," he said. "It calms the room, reminds everyone that we seek fairness and peace."

Another member added, "House visits are crucial. We counsel families, speak with respected elders, and guide them to find their own solutions."

Their approach was deeply community-oriented. They highlighted five key techniques: beginning with

THE TRI-JUSTICE SYSTEM IN ACTION: MY PERSONAL JOURNEY THROUGH LEGAL PLURALISM IN 15 BARMM BARANGAYS

a prayer, personal house visits and counseling, a brief but impactful opening message from the Lupon chair, the involvement of community elders, and coordination with relevant agencies. These strategies, they explained, had not only resolved disputes but also strengthened social ties.

As the discussion unfolded and more stories were shared, Ma'am Jolina, the team leader from the MILG Provincial Office leaned over and whispered, "Sir, time's up. We need to head to the next barangay." I nodded in agreement, although I wished we had more time to hear the rest of their experiences.

After a hearty lunch, prepared with the utmost hospitality, we bid farewell to the barangay chairman and his team. Their warmth lingered as we made our way back to Lamitan City, the day's lessons etched in our minds.

This visit to Tumahubong was more than just a formal engagement—it was a reminder that the true strength of a community lies in its ability to listen, adapt, and resolve from within.

*****

Story 18

FOR MALINIS, IT'S CAREFULLY CRAFTED

With time slipping away, we left Barangay Tumahubong in Sumisip Municipality and made our way back to Lamitan City. Our final stop awaited—the last of 15 barangays we were visiting in the entire

THE TRI-JUSTICE SYSTEM IN ACTION: MY PERSONAL JOURNEY THROUGH LEGAL PLURALISM IN 15 BARMM BARANGAYS

Bangsamoro Autonomous Region in Muslim Mindanao (BARMM).

As we drove, I turned to my teammate and said, "We're almost there. One last visit, then the ferry."

"Feels like a long day," they replied, "but it'll be worth it."

In less than an hour, we arrived at Barangay Malinis, nestled in the heart of Lamitan City. I had always assumed that Isabela City was predominantly Christian, while Lamitan was largely Yakan. I turned out to be wrong.

As we pulled up to the barangay hall at 2 p.m., the energetic chairwoman, along with her team of officials, welcomed us with warm smiles and eager handshakes.

"Welcome! We've been waiting for you since lunchtime," she said, her energy immediately brightening the room despite our delayed arrival.

"Sorry to keep you waiting," I said with a sheepish smile. "We drove straight from Sumisip. We're excited to hear about your work here."

During our focus group discussion (FGD) with the chairperson, some Lupon members, and other officials, the diversity of the barangay quickly became apparent.

"Our community is a mix," the chairwoman explained. "Mostly settlers, but we also have Yakan,

Tausug, and a few other Moro groups—Maranao, Iranun, Badjao. We even have some non-Moro indigenous peoples like the Subanen."

I was listening intently when she added, "It's the diversity that makes us stronger, but also, sometimes, a little more complicated when it comes to settling disputes."

It was then that she outlined the Lupong Tagapamayapa's methods for resolving conflicts. I leaned in as she described the thoughtful, culturally sensitive techniques they used:

"Every settlement starts with a prayer," she began. "We ask God to give wisdom to both parties so they can leave the proceedings at peace."

One of the Lupon members nodded in agreement. "It sets the right tone. People are calmer when they feel spiritually grounded."

"After the prayer," the chairwoman continued, "we explain the house rules. Both sides get time to speak, no interruptions. And believe me, no yelling. Phones are silent too. It's all about respect."

"That makes sense," I responded, thinking of how easily emotions can run high in disputes.

"We even have interpreters," she added with a smile. "If someone doesn't speak the local dialect or needs sign language, we make sure they understand everything. Everyone deserves to be heard."

"What about when emotions flare up?" I asked.

THE TRI-JUSTICE SYSTEM IN ACTION: MY PERSONAL JOURNEY THROUGH LEGAL PLURALISM IN 15 BARMM BARANGAYS

"Oh, we're prepared for that!" she chuckled. "We offer water and candies if things get too heated. It's amazing what a little sweetness can do to calm people down."

The chairwoman also chimed in, "And after a successful mediation, we give them a miniature Bible or Qur'an. It's like saying, 'Go forward with God's blessing.'"

This gesture particularly impressed me. "That's innovative," I said. "It reminds me of the concept of *yamīn*—swearing by the Qur'an—as part of the Shari'ah and customary laws. I've read about this in the Sulu and Luwaran Codes."

The chairwoman nodded. "Yes, exactly! It's our way of showing that this resolution is sacred. Both parties leave with a reminder of their commitment."

She then went on to explain how they sometimes involved external agencies for extra support. "We bring in the CSWD, the police, or even the health office when needed. Everyone has their role in making sure the resolution sticks."

"And after the settlement?" I asked.

"Afterwards, we always encourage a handshake or even a hug. It's symbolic," she said. "It means the fight is truly over."

A quiet moment followed, the weight of her words sinking in. Then she pointed to a small corner of the room. "That's our 'Calm Corner'. If someone needs privacy to talk or just calm down, we use that space. Sometimes, people just need a few moments to cool off."

It was a thoughtful touch—one of many that showed the depth of their dedication. She also explained how, in cases involving indigenous peoples, they invite tribal leaders to guide the proceedings.

"We make sure to respect their traditions," she said. "Sometimes it involves customary ceremonies like the giving of *Sarah* or a recitation of *Duwaa*. It's about keeping the process culturally respectful."

As our conversation deepened, Ma'am Jolina, the team leader from the MILG Provincial Office, glanced at her watch. "I hate to interrupt," she said softly, "but we really need to wrap up if we're going to catch the ferry."

The chairwoman smiled warmly. "Before you go, please join us for an early dinner. It's just at the next barangay building."

We gratefully accepted, sharing a simple but heartwarming meal that perfectly capped off the visit.

As we made the drive back to Isabela City, the roads seemed to blur as the events of the day replayed in my mind.

The community we had just left had a way of handling disputes that was both practical and profound—deeply rooted in cultural traditions yet open to innovation.

After snapping a few final photos at the pier, we bid farewell to Ma'am Jolina and her colleagues.

As the Montenegro sea vessel sliced through the waves, heading toward Zamboanga, I found myself reflecting on everything.

"In a world as diverse as Basilan," I thought, "peace is not just a hope. It's a deliberate, carefully crafted reality."

*****

Epilogue
RETRACING 3 PILLARS OF BARANGAY JUSTICE IN BARMM

As the sun bathed the tarmac of Zamboanga Airport in a soft golden hue, I sat with a cup of coffee in hand, waiting for my flight to Davao City. While the

THE TRI-JUSTICE SYSTEM IN ACTION: MY PERSONAL JOURNEY THROUGH LEGAL PLURALISM IN 15 BARMM BARANGAYS

hum of travelers and the gentle clinking of silverware echoed around me, my mind drifted far from the bustling predeparture area.

Instead, I found myself retracing the rich stories of conflict resolution woven into the 15 barangays of the Bangsamoro Autonomous Region in Muslim Mindanao (BARMM) I have just visited. These stories, filled with tradition, community, and faith, had left an indelible mark on me.

"The key to resolving disputes is understanding where people come from—both in spirit and in law," an elder from a barangay had said during one of our interviews. His words echoed in my thoughts as I sipped my coffee, reflecting on the diverse mediation techniques that each barangay had shared with me.

The focus group discussions dive deep into the amicable settlement techniques and best practices employed by these 15 barangays scattered across the BARMM. From the mainland provinces to the island provinces of Basilan to Tawi-Tawi, the integration of the tri-justice system—Philippine legal statutes, Moro Islamic laws (Shari'ah and *'adat*), and the Indigenous Peoples' Tribal Justice System—provided a framework that was as unique as it was profound.

Take all the barangays, for instance. Their mediation process is not just about resolving conflict; it's about healing. "Before we talk, we pray," the barangay chairperson had explained. "We ask for guidance and strength." The mediation begins with prayers and invocations, setting a solemn and respectful tone. A particular dispute I witnessed involved a land conflict between two families, which ended with the planting of a tree. "The tree symbolizes growth and new beginnings," a Lupon member had said, handing a sapling to the families. It wasn't just a settlement—it was a symbolic gesture rooted in faith and community.

In another barangay, where Islamic and customary laws work hand in hand, the integration of *'adat* (customary law) ensures that every decision feels both legally binding and spiritually fulfilling. As one community leader put it, "It is not enough to settle disputes in court; we must also settle them in our hearts." This deep respect for both law and tradition fosters a unique sense of justice that resonates deeply within the community.

Another standout example came from yet another barangay. There, after every dispute settlement, both parties gather at the "Well of Forgiveness" to symbolically release their anger by tossing stones into the well. "When the stone sinks," explained a Lupon member, "so does our resentment." A tangible act of forgiveness, the well serves as a powerful reminder that true resolution comes from letting go of the past.

Each barangay had its own rituals and customs. In one barangay, disputes were handled in a sacred room known as Mékétéfu Sébéy, a sanctuary for prayer before any mediation begins. "This room is a place of peace," one lady Lupon member shared. "It's where we ask God to open our minds and soften our hearts." The altar inside the room, shared by both Muslims and Christians, underscored the barangay's commitment to spiritual preparation as a vital part of the mediation process.

Even the smallest gestures carried weight. In a certain barangay, after disputes were settled, a 'Letter of Friendship' was exchanged—a written promise to maintain peace. "This letter is more than words on paper," a local mediator told me. "It's a commitment to each other, to the community, to harmony."

As I looked out the airplane window, the green landscapes below began to blur into the distance, much like the distinct yet interconnected mediation practices I had witnessed across BARMM. The flight from Zamboanga to Davao was only an hour, but my mind was still processing the deep wisdom shared by these communities.

One observation struck me most: the powerful blend of tradition and law that still shapes the conflict resolution practices in barangays with dominant Moro and Indigenous Peoples (IP) populations. However, not everything was without its challenges. Many Lupon members, tasked with mediating disputes, often found themselves confused about jurisdiction, especially in marital cases. One official had remarked, "We know the laws, but sometimes it's hard to draw the line between what's cultural, what's religious, and what's legal."

This blend of legal systems—while often beautiful in its harmony—also highlighted the need for more structured legal training. As I recalled these observations, I thought back to a conversation with a community leader who admitted, "We are good at talking to our people, but the law is something we are still learning to navigate."

As the plane touched down in Davao, I realized that the lessons I had gathered from these barangays were more than just data points for a training manual. They were a reminder that in the heart of every community lies the power to heal, to forgive, and to grow.

In the end, true justice isn't found solely in the words of the law but in the traditions, the people, and the quiet, powerful acts of reconciliation that stitch the fabric of peace together.

The journey had not just been about discovering techniques; it had been about witnessing the enduring strength of community-driven justice.

*****

ABOUT THE AUTHOR

Recipient of 13th International Farabi Award (2022) on Humanities and Islamic Studies, **Mansoor Limba** is a writer, translator, university professor, chess trainer, blogger, and publisher. He is a Shari'ah Counselor-at-Law (SCL), PhD holder in International Relations, and BA holder in Islamic Studies who writes and translates books (Persian into English and Filipino, English into Filipino) on such subjects as international politics, history, political philosophy, intra-faith and interfaith relations, preventing and countering violent extremism (PCVE), cultural heritage, Islamic finance, jurisprudence (*fiqh*), scholastic theology (*'ilm al-kalam*), Qur'anic sciences, hadith, ethics, and mysticism.

Limba is a KAICIID International Dialogue Centre Fellow and an alumnus of Clingendael (Netherlands Institute of International Relations) on Negotiation and Mediation in Conflict Resolution. He is also a columnist of Mindanews online news magazine (www.mindanews.com).

As an aspiring entrepreneur, Limba has opened ElziStyle Bookshop (elzistyle.com) to publish his written and translation works. As a financial education advocate, he has founded and maintains www.MuslimandMoney.com. As a certified chess trainer and Arena Candidate Master (ACM), he has established Cotabato City Chess Academy (CCCA) to teach chess to young players for the formation of core values and the blossoming of their academic and lifelong skills.

Have an experience with his multidisciplinary taste by visiting his blog at https://mlimba.com and financial literary advocacy at https://muslimandmoney.com and buying his eBooks at https://www.elzistyle.com.

OTHER BOOKS BY THE AUTHOR

Please visit your favorite book retailer to discover other books by Mansoor Limba:

Written Works
The Power of International Quds Day in the Cyberspace, https://amzn.to/34xW2cU
My Tehran Diary, https://amzn.to/3GuLN6z
Light Moments in Vienna, https://amzn.to/3u8DsCM
Muslim Couple and Money: 8 Practical Financial Tips for Newlywed Muslim Couples, https://amzn.to/3usheMc
12 Financial Stories for Muslim Kids, https://amzn.to/3KsO70P
Muslim and Debt: 5 Practical Steps to Freedom from Debt, https://amzn.to/3Gnn3x3
Kabuntalan through the Centuries: A Narrative of History and Culture, https://www.elzistyle.com/product/kabuntalan-through-the-centuries
The Hermeneutics of Violent Extremism in Mindanao, https://amzn.to/3qKpCEI
Mutahhari is Mutahhari: The Making of a Thinker, https://amzn.to/3AXguAa
'mBayuka Tanu! Maguindanaon *Bayuk* Transcription, Transcription, and Annotation, https://amzn.to/3uJMjLH
How to Shari'ah-compliantly Invest in the Philippine Stock Market: Beginner's Step-by-Step Guide, https://amzn.to/3ATj6QV
Financial Literacy for Muslim Teens: 12 Short Stories of Empowerment, https://amzn.to/4eBTyJf

Translation Works
Imam Khomeini, Ethics and Politics
Freedom: The Unstated Facts and Points, https://amzn.to/3J37fkx

Imam Khomeini and the International System
Imam Khomeini and the Muslim World, https://amzn.to/34uCzK9
Sahifeh-ye Imam: An Anthology of Imam Khomeini's Speeches, Messages, Interviews, Decrees, Religious Permissions and Letters (Volume 20), https://amzn.to/3umnPIe
Sahifeh-ye Imam: An Anthology of Imam Khomeini's Speeches, Messages, Interviews, Decrees, Religious Permissions and Letters (Volume 21), https://amzn.to/3umnPIe
An Overview of the Mahdi's Government, https://amzn.to/3uI42TV
The Radiance of the Secrets of Prayer, https://amzn.to/35RETeY
The Qur'an as Reflected in *Nahj al-Balaghah*
In the Presence of the Beloved: Commentaries on *Du'a' al-Iftitah*, *Du'a' Abu Hamzah al-Thumali* and *Du'a' Makarim al-Akhlaq*
A Commentary on Prayer, https://amzn.to/32Y1aGL
A Cursory Glance at the Theory of *Wilayat al-Faqih*
Training and Education in Islam
The Theory of Knowledge: An Islamic Perspective, https://amzn.to/3AWZ7iZ
Islamic Political Theory, Volume 1 (Legislation)
Islamic Political Theory, Volume 2 (Statecraft), https://amzn.to/34CQjTi
Investigations and Challenges: Discourses on Current Cultural, Sociopolitical and Religious Issues
An Introduction to *Hadith*: History and Sources, https://amzn.to/3Hwq7Im
Introduction to the Sciences of the Qur'an, https://amzn.to/3Kquhn9
The Qur'an and Immunity from Distortion, https://amzn.to/3HxCdRu
Discursive Theology, Volume 1, https://amzn.to/3GnnIi1
Discursive Theology, Volume 2, https://amzn.to/3FFACra
Philosophy of Religion, https://amzn.to/35GhjBG
Fitrah: Man's Natural Disposition, https://amzn.to/3GtlCNm

Philosophy of Ethics, https://amzn.to/3ur75iY
Hijab and Mental Health, https://amzn.to/3HwztUr
Risalah Liqa' Allah: A Treatise on the Stages of Mystical Wayfaring toward the Station of Beatific Vision, https://amzn.to/34W5dUD
The Revival of Islamic Thought, https://amzn.to/3LdQKEo
Risalah Ma'rifat Allah: An Exposition of Imam 'Ali ibn Musa al-Rida's ('a) Sermon on the Gnosis of Allah, https://amzn.to/3FJQn0o
Misbah al-Shari'ah: A Commentary on *Misbah al-Shari'ah* (*Lantern of the Path*) Attributed to Imam Ja'far al-Sadiq ('a), https://amzn.to/3tGautW
Esoteric Traditions: An Exposition of Imam Musa ibn Ja'far's ('a) Mystical and Philosophical Traditions, https://amzn.to/3AXUrt9
Imam al-Rida's ('a) Esoteric Traditions: An Exposition of Selected Traditions from *'Uyun Akhbar al-Rida*, https://amzn.to/3gr1bWY
Risalah Sayr wa Suluk: An Exposition of Sayyid Bahr al-'Ulum's Treatise on Mystical Wayfaring, https://amzn.to/3gGrskl
Scientific Approach in Translating and Interpreting the Noble Qur'an and Traditions, https://amzn.to/3uocLdD
Tafsir-e Rushan: An Elucidated Exegesis of the Qur'an, Volume 1
The Issue of Ḥijāb, https://amzn.to/3rmQ7jG
Replies to Critiques of the Book 'The Issue of Ḥijāb, https://amzn.to/3gf7GMo
The Mysticism of Hafiz by Murtada Mutahhari, https://amzn.to/3XfkSoT
Banking and Insurance in Islam by Murtada Mutahhari, https://amzn.to/3Dr8tFP

CONNECT WITH THE AUTHOR

I really appreciate you reading my book! Here are my social media coordinates:

Add me on Facebook: http://facebook.com/mansoor.limba

Follow me on Twitter: http://twitter.com/mansoor_limba

Follow me on Instagram:
https://www.instagram.com/m_limba

Pin my photos on Pinterest:
https://www.pinterest.ph/mansoorlimba

Favorite my Smashwords author page:
https://www.smashwords.com/profile/view/mlimba

Favorite my Amazon author page:
www.amazon.com/author/mansoorlimba

Connect on LinkedIn:
https://ph.linkedin.com/pub/mansoor-limba/b6/383/720

Subscribe to my blog: http://www.mlimba.com

Subscribe to my channel:
http://www.youtube.com/c/wayfaringwithmansoor

Visit my financial literacy website:
https://www.muslimandmoney.com

Purchase my books: https://www.elzistyle.com

www.ingramcontent.com/pod-product-compliance
Lightning Source LLC
Chambersburg PA
CBHW070143230526
45471CB00002B/496